Eli
Manning

ABDO
Publishing Company

A Big Buddy Book
by **Sarah Tieck**

VISIT US AT
www.abdopublishing.com

Published by ABDO Publishing Company, 8000 West 78th Street, Edina, Minnesota 55439.

Copyright © 2009 by Abdo Consulting Group, Inc. International copyrights reserved in all countries. No part of this book may be reproduced in any form without written permission from the publisher. Buddy Books™ is a trademark and logo of ABDO Publishing Company.

Printed in the United States.

Coordinating Series Editor: Rochelle Baltzer
Contributing Editors: Heidi M.D. Elston, Megan M. Gunderson, Marcia Zappa
Graphic Design: Maria Hosley
Cover Photograph: AP Photo: Bill Kostroun
Interior Photographs/Illustrations: AP Photo: AP Photo (page 13), Tammie Arroyo (page 7), Gregory Bull (page 21), Chuck Burton (pages 5, 29), cwh (page 8), Morry Gash (page 29), Tony Gutierrez (pages 13, 16, 22), Rusty Kennedy (page 20), Bill Kostoun (page 19), John Marshall Mantel (page 10), David J. Phillip (page 23), Rogelio Solis (pages 15, 17), Charlie Riedel (page 24), The Courier, Matt Stamey (page 9); Getty Images: NFL/Tom Berg (page 19), PGA/Sam Greenwood (page 13), WireImage/Jamie McCarthy (page 27).

Library of Congress Cataloging-in-Publication Data

Tieck, Sarah, 1976-
  Eli Manning / Sarah Tieck.
      p. cm. -- (Big buddy biographies)
  Includes index.
  ISBN 978-1-60453-124-4
  1. Manning, Eli, 1981- 2. Football players--United States--Biography--Juvenile literature.
  3. Quarterbacks (Football)--United States--Biography--Juvenile literature. I. Title.

GV939.M289T54 2009
796.332092--dc22
[B]
                              2008009362

Contents

Football Star

Eli Manning is famous for his sports skills. He plays football in the National Football League (NFL). Eli is a talented, popular quarterback for the New York Giants.

Eli's brother and father are famous quarterbacks, too. Quarterbacks are known for their passing skills. They often help their teams score.

Where in the World?

Arkansas

Texas

Louisiana

Mississippi

New Orleans

GULF OF
MEXICO

N
W   E
S

Family Ties

Elisha Nelson "Eli" Manning was born on January 3, 1981, in New Orleans, Louisiana. His parents are Archie and Olivia Manning. Eli has two older brothers, Peyton and Cooper.

Archie, Peyton, Cooper, and
Eli love to play football together.
Archie taught his sons to play when
they were growing up.

Growing Up

Eli spent his childhood in New Orleans. His family loved football. Eli learned football skills by practicing with his father and brothers.

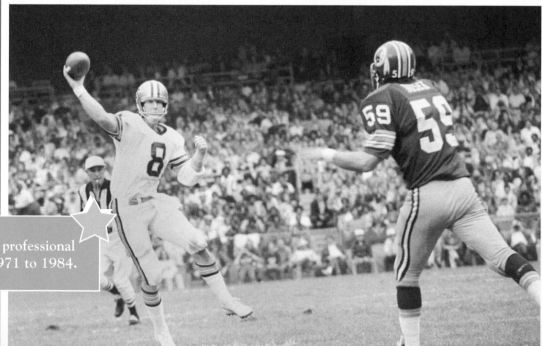

Archie (*left*) was a professional quarterback from 1971 to 1984.

Eli *(left)* and his family run Manning Passing Academy in the summer. This four-day camp helps high school football players improve their skills.

People started to notice Eli's football skills in high school. His parents always cheered him on.

Because he was a **professional** football player, Archie traveled often. So young Eli became close with his mother.

When Eli had trouble reading in first grade, Olivia helped him improve. They also spent time together going out for pizza or catfish dinners.

Football Family

Eli comes from a famous football family. Archie played with the New Orleans Saints for 11 seasons. He taught his sons to love the game.

In high school, Cooper was a wide receiver. However, he got hurt and had to stop playing football.

Peyton played football in high school and college. Then, he became an Indianapolis Colts quarterback.

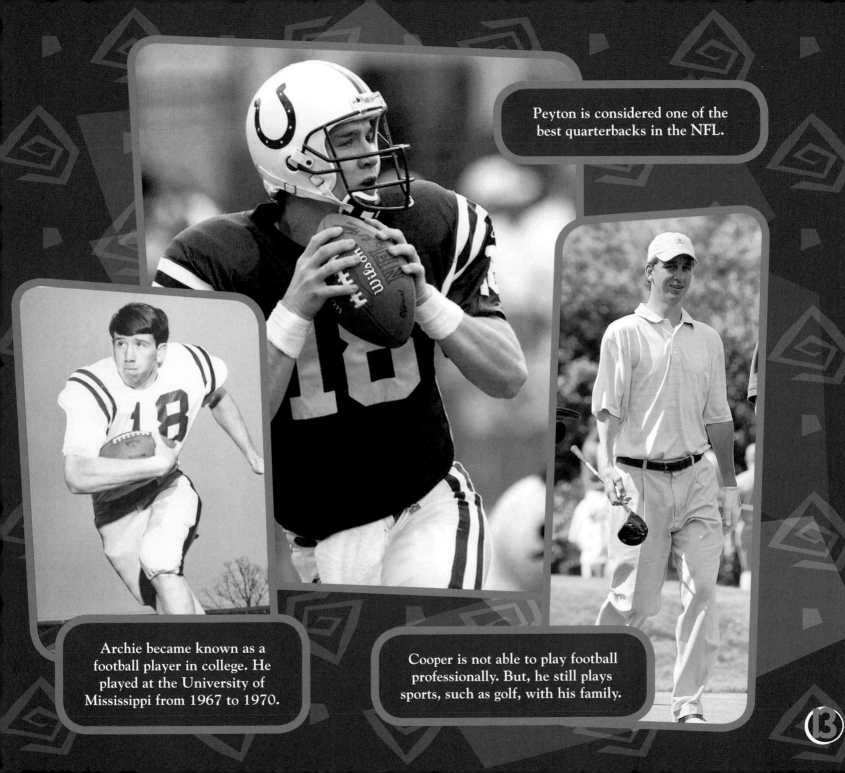

Peyton is considered one of the best quarterbacks in the NFL.

Archie became known as a football player in college. He played at the University of Mississippi from 1967 to 1970.

Cooper is not able to play football professionally. But, he still plays sports, such as golf, with his family.

College Years

Like his brothers, Eli played football in high school. And like his father, Eli attended the University of Mississippi in Oxford, Mississippi. There, he became a quarterback as his father had.

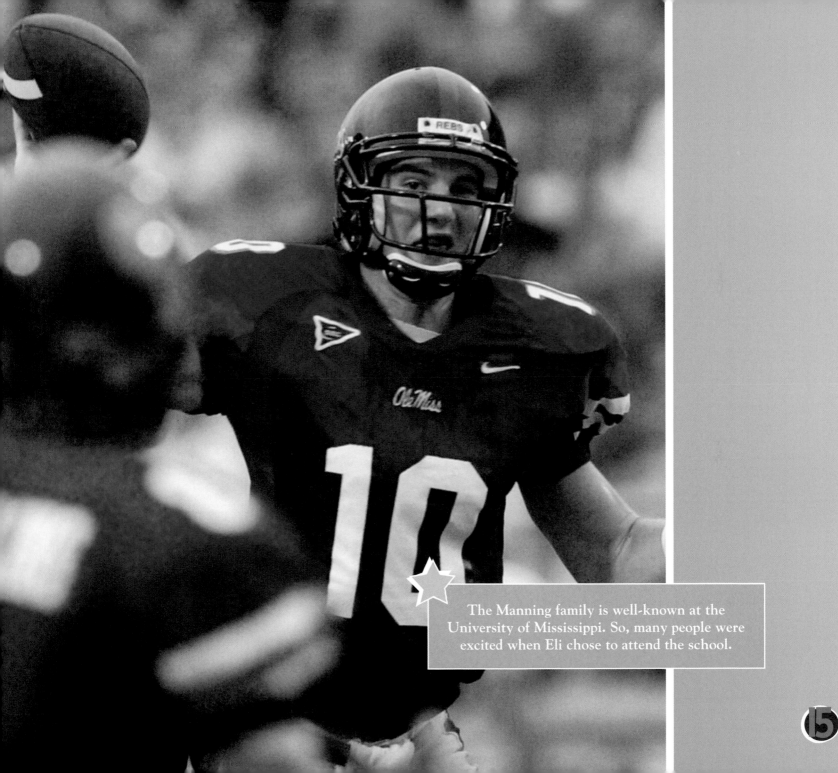

The Manning family is well-known at the University of Mississippi. So, many people were excited when Eli chose to attend the school.

Ole Miss was chosen to play in the 2004 Cotton Bowl. Eli and his teammates beat Oklahoma State!

During college, Eli won many awards for his football skills. In 2003, he was given the Maxwell Award. This was for being the country's best player.

That year, Eli also received the Johnny Unitas Golden Arm Award. Outstanding quarterbacks receive this award for having good character and leadership skills.

Going Pro

After graduating from college, Eli decided to play professional football. During the 2004 NFL draft, the San Diego Chargers chose Eli. Later that day, he was traded to the New York Giants.

Eli was the number one pick in the 2004 NFL draft. Peyton *(far left)*, Olivia *(left)*, and Archie *(right)* were there to support him.

Coach Tom Coughlin *(left)* and general manager Ernie Accorsi *(right)* were very happy Eli joined the New York Giants.

Did you know...

Football teams have several players for each position. The starters begin the game. Backups play if the starters are hurt or playing poorly.

Eli's first season as an NFL player was 2004. That season, the Giants lost eight games in a row! Eli helped his team win the last game of the season.

In 2005, quarterback Kurt Warner left the Giants. So, Eli became the starting quarterback. He helped his team have a winning season. However, the Giants did not do well in the **play-offs**.

Football is a tough sport. Players tackle,
or bring down, each other to get the ball.

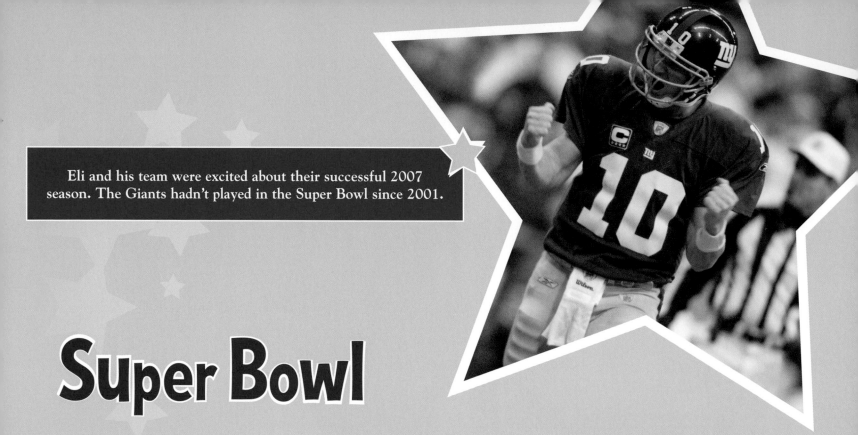

Eli and his team were excited about their successful 2007 season. The Giants hadn't played in the Super Bowl since 2001.

Super Bowl

Toward the end of the 2007 season, the Giants began to stand out. They made it into the 2008 NFL **play-offs**. During the play-offs, Eli's team beat the Tampa Bay Buccaneers, the Dallas Cowboys, and the Green Bay Packers.

These wins meant that the Giants would play in the 2008 Super Bowl! The Super Bowl is the **championship** game of the NFL. Each year, the two top teams play to win this event.

In 2007, the Giants played well in some games and poorly in others. So, people were surprised when they won in the play-offs. This is called an upset.

Eli helped the Giants win the Super Bowl in 2008. He threw two touchdowns late in the game. A touchdown is a way to score six points by having possession of the football in the end zone.

On February 3, 2008, the New York Giants played the New England Patriots in the Super Bowl. Record numbers of fans watched the game on television. The Patriots were undefeated. So, most people expected them to win.

But, the Giants pulled off a win! The final score was 17 to 14. Some say this was a historic game!

Where in the World?

New York

Massachusetts

Connecticut

Rhode Island

Hoboken

Pennsylvania

New Jersey

Maryland

ATLANTIC OCEAN

Delaware

Family Man

In April 2008, Eli married Abby McGrew. Eli and Abby live in Hoboken, New Jersey. Eli spends a lot of time with his family. He likes to shop for antiques with his wife and mother. And, he golfs with his father and brothers.

Did you know...

Abby works in fashion in New York.

Eli and Abby were married on a beach in Mexico. They met when they were students at Ole Miss.

27

Eli practices his game to stay prepared for the start of each new football season.

Buzz

In 2008, Eli was named the Super Bowl's MVP. He is a rising star! Fans expect great things from Eli Manning.

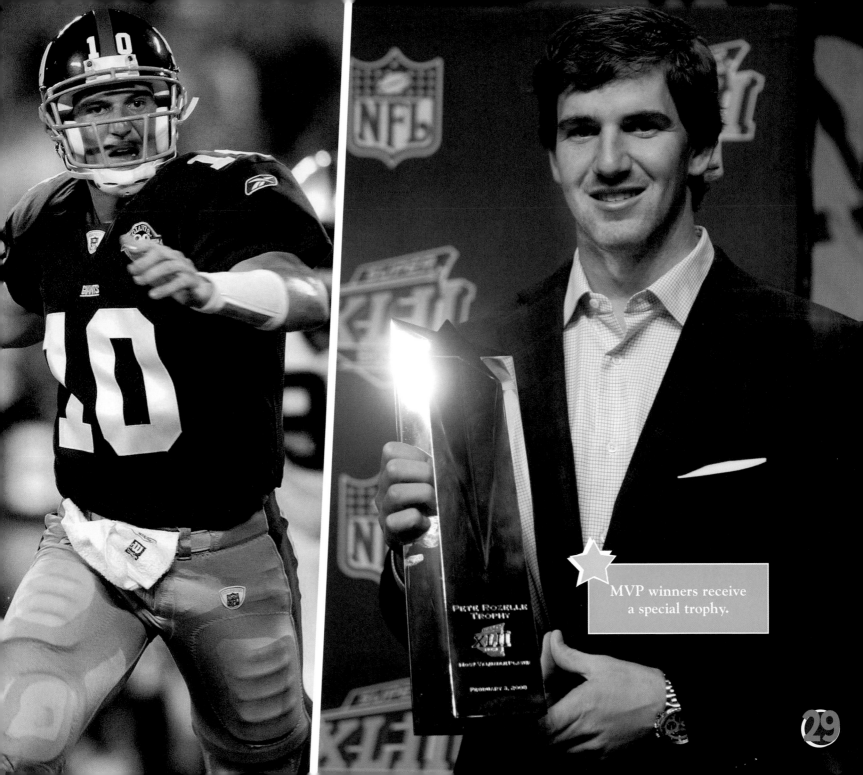

MVP winners receive a special trophy.

PETE ROZELLE
TROPHY

XLII

MOST VALUABLE PLAYER

FEBRUARY 3, 2008

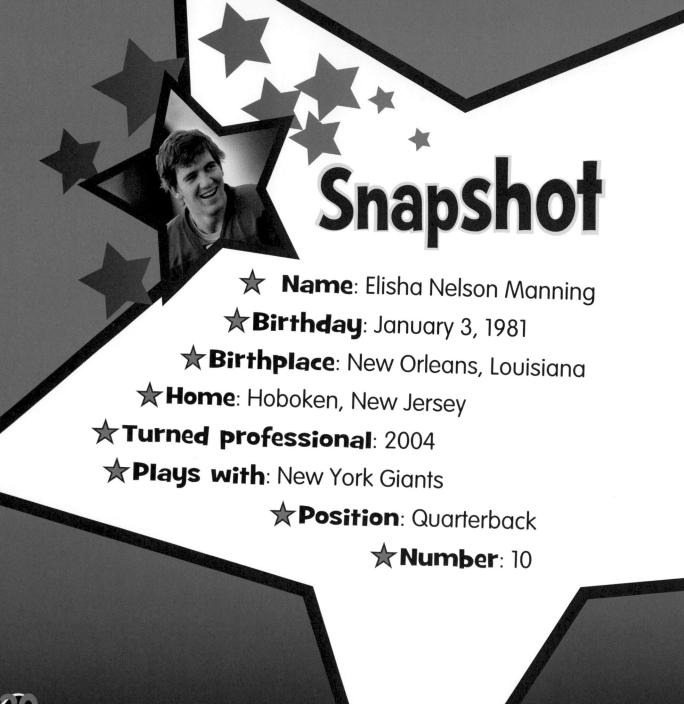

Snapshot

⭐ **Name**: Elisha Nelson Manning

⭐ **Birthday**: January 3, 1981

⭐ **Birthplace**: New Orleans, Louisiana

⭐ **Home**: Hoboken, New Jersey

⭐ **Turned professional**: 2004

⭐ **Plays with**: New York Giants

⭐ **Position**: Quarterback

⭐ **Number**: 10

Important Words

antique (an-TEEK) an old item that has collectible value.

championship a game or a match held to find a first place winner.

draft an event during which sports teams choose beginning players.

play-off a series of games leading to a final match to find a winner.

professional (pruh-FEHSH-nuhl) working for money rather than for pleasure.

Web Sites

To learn more about Eli Manning, visit ABDO Publishing Company on the World Wide Web. Web sites about Eli Manning are featured on our Book Links page. These links are routinely monitored and updated to provide the most current information available.

www.abdopublishing.com

Index